ADA LOVELACE
Biography for kids

INSPIRING STORY OF GENIUS AND THE WORLD'S FIRST PROGRAMMER FOR YOUNG READERS

BRIGHT FUTURE BOOKS

© 2024 **Bright Future Books**. All rights reserved.

No part of this publication may be reproduced, distributed, or transmitted in any form or by any means, including photocopying, recording, or other electronic or mechanical methods, without the prior written permission of the publisher, except in the case of brief quotations embodied in critical reviews and certain other noncommercial uses permitted by copyright law.

Table Of Content

Table Of Content 3
Introduction 4
Chapter 1 7
Chapter 2 11
Chapter 3 14
Chapter 4 17
Chapter 5 23
Chapter 6 29
Chapter 7 34
Chapter 8 39
Chapter 9 45
Decode a Secret Message! 51
Questions 53
Glossary 61
Timeline of Ada's Life 68

Introduction

Meet Ada Lovelace: A Pioneer in Computing

Have you ever played a game on a tablet or asked a smart speaker a question? We use computers every day, but did you know that the idea of computers started a long, long time ago? Let me introduce you to Ada Lovelace—the amazing woman who imagined computers before they even existed!

Ada lived almost 200 years ago in a time when there were no TVs, no internet, and not even light bulbs! People traveled by horse and wrote letters by hand. But Ada was different; she loved numbers, puzzles, and dreaming up big ideas. While others were riding in carriages, she was imagining machines that could think and calculate.

One day, Ada met an inventor named Charles Babbage. He was working on a giant machine full of gears and levers.

Most people didn't understand his invention, but Ada did! She saw something special—a future where machines could do much more than just crunch numbers.

Guess what? Ada wrote the first instructions for these machines—what we now call a computer program! That's why she's known as the world's first computer programmer. Pretty cool, right?

In this book, we're going to dive into Ada's exciting world. We'll explore how her big dreams and love for math changed the way we live today. So get ready to travel back in time and meet the girl who saw the future of computers before anyone else.

Are you excited? Let's go on an adventure with Ada Lovelace!

Chapter 1

Ada's Famous Parents

Imagine having a dad who's a superstar poet and a mom who's a math whiz! That's exactly how life began for Ada Lovelace.

Ada's father was **Lord Byron**, one of the most famous poets in the world. People loved his exciting and adventurous poems. He was like a rock star of poetry in the 1800s! But here's a surprising fact: Ada never really knew her dad. He left England when she was just a baby, and they never met again. Even so, his love for creativity might have sparked something in Ada.

Her mother, **Lady Annabella Milbanke Byron**, was brilliant with numbers. She was nicknamed the "Princess of Parallelograms" because of her love for mathematics—how cool is that? Lady Byron wanted Ada to have the best education possible, especially in math and science. She believed that learning would help Ada grow into a smart and independent woman.

Growing up with such remarkable parents, Ada had both creativity and logic in her genes. It was the perfect mix for someone who would one day imagine the future of computers!

Early Life and Childhood Adventures

Ada was not your ordinary girl. From a young age, she was curious about everything around her. She loved asking questions like "How does the clock work?" or "Can we build a machine that flies?"

Speaking of flying, when Ada was just 12 years old, she became obsessed with the idea of flight. She studied birds to figure out how they stayed up in the air. Ada filled notebooks with sketches of wings, feathers, and even designs for a flying machine powered by steam! She called it her "Flyology" project. Imagine building your own airplane before airplanes were even invented!

But life wasn't always easy for Ada. She often got sick and had to stay in bed for long periods. Did that stop her? No way! Ada used that time to read books, solve math problems, and dream up new inventions. Her imagination knew no bounds.

Ada's mother made sure she had the best teachers. She learned mathematics, science, languages, and even music. Back then, girls were usually taught things like sewing and singing, but Ada was different. She dove into subjects that were mostly studied by boys. And guess what? She excelled!

One of her tutors said that Ada had "an amazing head for mathematics." She didn't just learn from books; she wanted to understand how the world worked. Whether it was exploring gardens, watching stars, or tinkering with gadgets, Ada turned every moment into an adventure.

Ada's childhood was full of learning, creativity, and big dreams. Little did she know, these adventures were just the beginning of an incredible journey that would change the world forever!

Isn't Ada's story fascinating? From her famous parents to her own daring ideas, she showed that curiosity and hard work can lead to amazing things. Get ready, because Ada's journey is just getting started!

Chapter 2

Discovering Math and Science

Ada Lovelace wasn't just any kid—she had a special sparkle when it came to numbers and science! While other children played with dolls or toy soldiers, Ada found joy in solving puzzles and exploring the wonders of the world.

From a young age, Ada was fascinated by how things worked. She would watch the rain and wonder how water droplets formed. She'd look at a clock and marvel at the gears moving inside. Ada's mind was always buzzing with questions!

One day, she asked her mother, "How does the sun shine?" Instead of giving a simple answer, her mother encouraged her to explore and find out. This led Ada to discover books about astronomy, the study of stars and planets. Imagine being eight years old and already curious about the universe!

Math became Ada's favorite subject. To her, numbers weren't just symbols on a page—they were like friends that helped explain the mysteries around her. She loved that math could solve problems and reveal hidden patterns.

Ada also enjoyed science experiments. She'd mix safe ingredients from the kitchen to see what would happen, like combining baking soda and vinegar to make a fizzy explosion! Her enthusiasm was contagious, and even her tutors were amazed by her eagerness to learn.

Chapter 3

Ada's Extraordinary Education

Back in the 1800s, most girls didn't get to study much math or science. But Ada was different, and her mother made sure she had the best education possible.

Ada had wonderful teachers who were experts in their fields. One of her tutors was Mary Somerville, a brilliant mathematician and scientist. Mary became a great friend and role model for Ada. She showed Ada that women could excel in science and make important discoveries.

Under Mary's guidance, Ada learned about algebra, geometry, and even calculus—subjects that were very advanced, especially for someone her age! Ada didn't just memorize formulas; she wanted to understand why they worked. She treated math like a grand adventure, exploring new ideas with excitement.

Ada also learned about mechanics, the study of how machines and physical forces work. She was intrigued by inventions like the steam engine, which powered trains and factories at the time. This interest would later help her understand complex machines like Charles Babbage's Analytical Engine.

But it wasn't all work and no play! Ada balanced her studies with music and art. She played the piano and enjoyed drawing. This mix of creativity and logic made her thinking unique. She could imagine amazing inventions and then figure out the math to make them possible!

Ada's education wasn't just about learning facts; it was about thinkiing differently. She combined her love for numbers with her big imagination, which set the stage for her incredible contributions to computing.

Isn't it inspiring how Ada's passion for learning led her to do extraordinary things? She showed that with curiosity and hard work, you can unlock the secrets of the universe. Who knows what amazing discoveries **you** might make one day?

Chapter 4

The Inventor Friend

Meeting Charles Babbage

Ada Lovelace was about to meet someone who would change her life forever—a brilliant inventor named Charles Babbage!

One day, when Ada was 17 years old, her mother took her to a grand party in London. But this wasn't just any party; it was a gathering of some of the smartest minds of the time—scientists, mathematicians, and inventors. Imagine a room buzzing with exciting ideas and discoveries waiting to happen!

At the party, Ada was introduced to Charles Babbage, a famous mathematician and inventor. He was much older than Ada, but age didn't matter when it came to sharing big ideas. Charles was working on something extraordinary, and Ada was eager to learn all about it.

Charles showed Ada a small model of his latest invention called the **Difference Engine**. It was a fascinating machine full of shiny brass gears and levers that could calculate math problems all by itself! While others saw a complex contraption, Ada saw magic in motion.

"How does it work?" Ada asked, her eyes wide with wonder.

Charles was delighted by her curiosity. He explained how the gears turned and how the machine could solve difficult calculations without making mistakes.

As they talked, Charles realized that Ada wasn't like most people—she truly understood the potential of his machine. Ada saw beyond what it was; she imagined what it could be. Charles nicknamed her the "Enchantress of Numbers" because of her remarkable ability to grasp mathematical concepts.

From that day on, Ada and Charles became great friends. They exchanged letters filled with ideas, dreams, and mathematical puzzles. Their friendship was the beginning of something incredible!

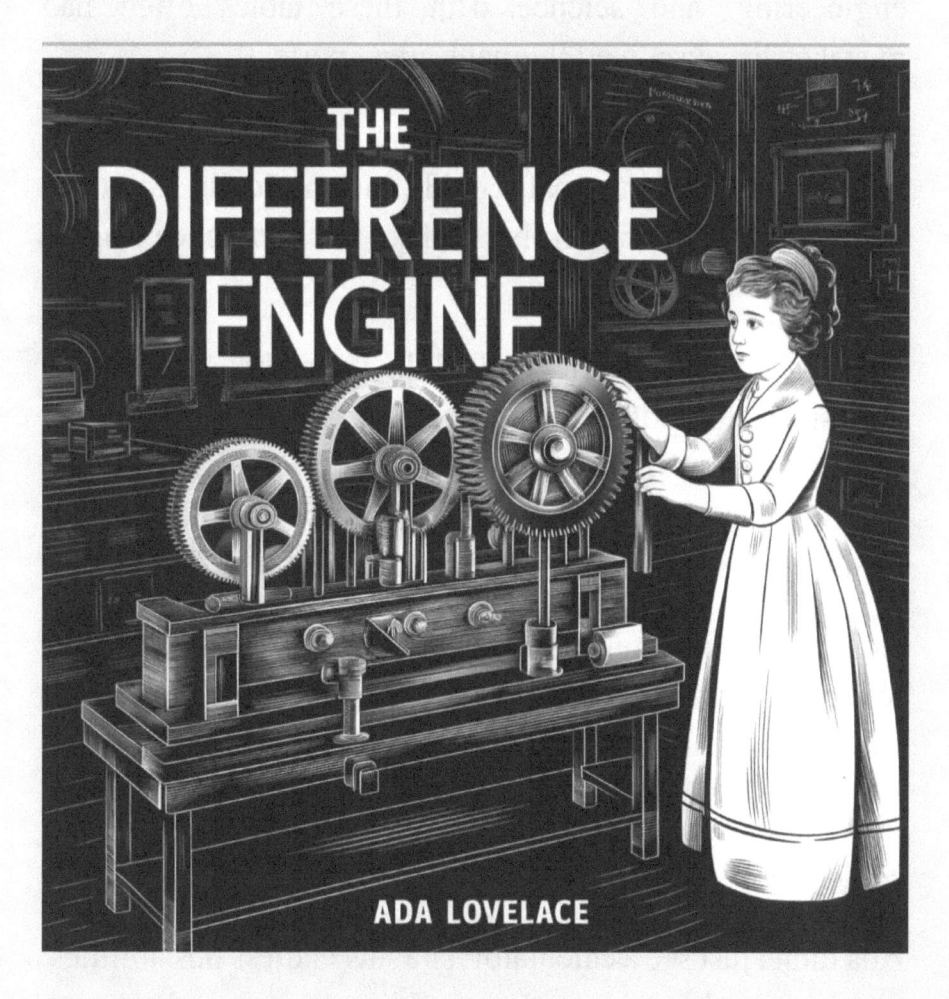

The Fascinating Difference Engine

Let's dive into the marvelous world of the **Difference Engine**, the invention that brought Ada and Charles together!

Back in the 1800s, doing math calculations was a big challenge. People used huge books filled with numbers called "mathematical tables" to help them with navigation, engineering, and science. But these tables often had mistakes because, well, humans aren't perfect!

Charles Babbage wanted to fix this problem. He dreamed of building a machine that could **automatically** calculate numbers without any errors. And so, the Difference Engine was born.

The Difference Engine looked like something out of a fantastical storybook! It was made up of thousands of gears, wheels, and rods, all working together in harmony. When you turned a crank, the gears would spin, and the machine would compute complex math problems in a flash.

Ada was absolutely fascinated. She visited Charles's workshop to see the machine in action. As the gears clicked and clacked, Ada's imagination began to whirl.

"Just think," she said, "if a machine can do math, what else could it do?"

Ada didn't just see a calculator; she saw endless possibilities. She imagined machines that could compose music, create art, or even think like a human—all by following a set of instructions!

Charles shared with her his plans for an even more advanced machine called the **Analytical Engine**. Unlike the Difference Engine, which could only do specific calculations, the Analytical Engine would be programmable—it could be told to do all sorts of tasks!

Ada's eyes sparkled with excitement. She realized that if they could write instructions—or programs—for the machine, it could solve problems beyond math. This idea was the seed that would grow into the concept of computer programming.

Together, Ada and Charles explored these groundbreaking ideas. Ada began to write down her thoughts on how the Analytical Engine could work and what it could achieve. She was venturing into a whole new world that no one had explored before!

Fun Fact: The Difference Engine was so ahead of its time that a full working model wasn't built until 150 years later, in 1991! And guess what? It worked exactly as Charles Babbage and Ada Lovelace had imagined.

Isn't it amazing how a chance meeting sparked a friendship that would change the world? Ada and Charles showed that when curiosity meets invention, the possibilities are endless. They dreamed big, asked questions, and weren't afraid to explore the unknown.

Who knows? Maybe you have a friend who will join you on your own adventures of discovery. Just like Ada and Charles, you might change the world someday!

Chapter 5

Imagining the Future

The Analytical Engine Explained

Get ready to journey into a world where imagination meets invention! Ada Lovelace and her friend Charles Babbage were about to unveil something truly extraordinary—the **Analytical Engine**.

So, what is the Analytical Engine? Imagine a gigantic mechanical machine, filled with gears, levers, and whirring parts, much like a colossal clock or a steampunk marvel from a fantasy story. This wasn't just any machine; it was designed to be the world's first **general-purpose computer**!

Unlike the Difference Engine, which could only perform specific calculations, the Analytical Engine was meant to be **programmable**. That means it could follow a set of instructions, called a program, to perform all sorts of mathematical tasks. Think of it like a robot that could do different jobs depending on the commands you gave it.

Here's how it worked:

- **Input:** The machine would receive instructions and data through punched cards. These cards had holes punched in specific patterns to represent different commands and numbers.
- **The Mill:** This was like the brain of the machine, where calculations happened. Charles called it the "mill" because it ground out answers like a mill grinds wheat into flour.
- **The Store:** This part held numbers and results, kind of like a memory bank.

- **Output:** After processing, the machine would produce results, perhaps printing them on paper or displaying them through dials.

Ada was fascinated by the Analytical Engine. She saw it as a magical device that could transform the way people worked with numbers and calculations. While others saw a complex machine, Ada saw endless possibilities.

She spent hours studying Charles's designs, asking questions like:

- "How can we make the machine solve different kinds of problems?"
- "What if we use the punched cards to tell the machine to do more than just math?"

Ada's curiosity led her to understand the Analytical Engine better than anyone else at the time—even Charles himself!

Ada's Vision Beyond Her Time

Ada didn't just understand the Analytical Engine; she **imagined** all the incredible things it could do—things that no one else had thought of yet.

She believed that the machine could handle not just numbers but **symbols, letters, and even music**! Ada thought that if you could find a way to represent things like musical notes or letters with numbers, the Analytical Engine could process them too.

In her own words, she wrote, "The Analytical Engine might compose elaborate and scientific pieces of music of any degree of complexity or extent." Imagine that—a machine creating music! This idea was absolutely mind-blowing in the 1800s.

Ada began to write detailed notes about the Analytical Engine, exploring its potential. She translated an article about the machine from French to English and added her own thoughts, which turned out to be even longer than the original article!

In her notes, Ada did something truly groundbreaking—she wrote the **first computer program**. She created a sequence of instructions that the Analytical Engine could follow to calculate a complex series of numbers known as Bernoulli numbers. This was the first time anyone had written a program for a machine, making Ada the world's first computer programmer!

But Ada's vision didn't stop there. She wondered:

- Could machines ever think like humans?
- What other tasks could machines be programmed to do?
- How might machines help us understand the world better?

Her ideas were so advanced that it took over a hundred years for technology to catch up!

Fun Fact: Ada loved the idea of flying machines. Remember her childhood "Flyology" project? She imagined that machines, like the Analytical Engine, could even help design aircraft one day!

Ada's insights were like a window into the future. She saw that machines could do so much more than just calculate—they could help us create, explore, and understand new things.

Today, we have computers that can compose music, draw pictures, play chess, and even help doctors diagnose illnesses. All these incredible advancements trace back to the ideas Ada had nearly two centuries ago!

Isn't it amazing how Ada Lovelace used her imagination and love for math to see possibilities that no one else did? She teaches us that with curiosity and creativity, we can dream up ideas that could shape the future.

So next time you use a computer, play a video game, or listen to music created by a digital artist, remember Ada—the girl who imagined it all before anyone else.

In this chapter, Ada's story shows us the power of thinking beyond what's in front of us. She combined her love for numbers with her wild imagination, proving that creativity and science can work together to make magic happen!

Chapter 6

Writing the First Program

Ada's Important Notes

Get ready to uncover how Ada Lovelace's big ideas turned into reality! After learning so much about Charles Babbage's Analytical Engine, Ada was bursting with thoughts she wanted to share with the world.

Around this time, a scientist wrote an article in French about the Analytical Engine. Ada was asked to **translate** it into English so more people could understand it. But Ada didn't stop at just translating—she added her own amazing ideas and explanations. In fact, her additions, called **"Ada's Notes,"** were three times longer than the original article!

In her notes, Ada explained how the Analytical Engine worked in a way that was easy to understand. She used examples and even imagined the machine creating music or art! Ada believed that the engine could do much more than just crunch numbers—it could follow **instructions** to perform all sorts of tasks.

Ada's Notes became a treasure trove of ideas about computing and what machines could achieve. She was painting a picture of the future, where machines and humans could work together to solve complex problems.

How She Created the First Algorithm

Now for the most exciting part—Ada wrote what is considered the world's **first computer program**!

An **algorithm** is like a recipe that tells a machine what steps to take to solve a problem. Just like you might follow a recipe to bake cookies, a machine follows an algorithm to complete a task.

Here's how Ada did it:

1. **Choosing a Challenge:** Ada decided to create a program to calculate something called **Bernoulli numbers**. These are special numbers in mathematics that are important but tricky to compute.
2. **Breaking It Down:** She took the complex math problem and broke it down into simple steps that the Analytical Engine could understand.
3. **Writing the Instructions:** Ada wrote out each step in detail, telling the machine exactly what to do at each point. She thought about how the gears and levers would move to perform each calculation.
4. **Using Punched Cards:** Back then, machines received instructions through **punched cards**—pieces of cardboard with holes punched in specific places. The pattern of holes represented different commands.
5. **Creating a Flowchart:** Ada even drew diagrams to show how the calculations would flow from one step to the next. This helped others visualize how the program worked.
6. **Double-Checking:** She went over her program carefully to make sure there were no mistakes. Accuracy was super important!

Even though the Analytical Engine was never built in her lifetime, Ada's program was a huge breakthrough. She showed that a machine could be programmed to carry out complex calculations—something that had never been done before!

Why Is This So Important?

Ada's work laid the foundation for modern computing. She was the first person to realize that machines could follow a set of instructions to perform tasks, which is exactly how computers work today!

Every time you play a video game, use a smartphone app, or watch a movie made with computer graphics, you're benefiting from programming—the field Ada helped create.

In this chapter, we see how Ada Lovelace used her love of math and creativity to write the first computer program. She showed that with imagination and careful planning, we can teach machines to help us in incredible ways.

Fun Fact: Ada's algorithm was so detailed that modern computer scientists have tested it, and it works! This shows how brilliant her work was, even by today's standards.

Isn't Ada's story inspiring? She proved that thinking differently and exploring new ideas can lead to amazing discoveries. Maybe one day, you'll write programs or invent machines that change the world too!

Keep Dreaming Big!

Just like Ada, you can combine your interests—whether it's math, art, science, or storytelling—to create something unique. The possibilities are endless when you let your imagination soar.

Chapter 7

Overcoming Challenges

Being a Woman in the 19th Century

Imagine living in a time when girls were told that they couldn't become scientists, engineers, or mathematicians just because they were girls! That's the world Ada Lovelace was born into in the 1800s.

Back then, society had very strict ideas about what women could and couldn't do. Girls were expected to focus on learning how to sew, play the piano, or host parties. Studying advanced subjects like math and science was considered "unladylike." Can you believe that?

But Ada was different. She **loved** numbers, puzzles, and discovering how things worked. She didn't let society's expectations stop her from following her passions. Still, being a girl interested in math wasn't easy.

Here are some of the challenges Ada faced:

- **Limited Education Opportunities:** Many schools and universities didn't allow women to attend. Ada was lucky that her mother supported her learning, but she still had to find private tutors because regular schools weren't an option.
- **Skepticism from Others:** People often didn't take Ada seriously. They thought a woman couldn't possibly understand complex subjects. Some even laughed at the idea of a female mathematician!
- **Social Restrictions:** Ada couldn't easily visit places like scientific societies or laboratories where new ideas were shared. These places were mostly for men, so she had to find other ways to learn and contribute.

But Ada didn't let these obstacles stop her. She was determined to pursue her love for math and science, no matter what others thought.

Ada's Determination and Courage

So, how did Ada overcome these challenges? With **determination** and a whole lot of **courage**!

Support from Her Mother: Ada's mother believed in her potential. She hired the best tutors to teach Ada math and science at home. This was unusual at the time, but it gave Ada the chance to learn and grow.

Finding Mentors: Ada connected with brilliant minds like Mary Somerville, one of the first women to be recognized as a scientist. Mary became Ada's friend and mentor, encouraging her to pursue her interests.

Hard Work and Persistence: Ada studied tirelessly. She didn't give up when things got tough. Even when she faced difficult math problems, she kept trying until she understood them.

Believing in Herself: Perhaps the most important thing was that Ada **believed in herself**. She knew that her ideas were valuable, and she didn't let negative opinions bring her down.

Making Her Voice Heard: When Ada wrote her famous Notes on the Analytical Engine, she didn't hide behind a pen name or let others take credit. She proudly shared her work with the world.

An Inspiring Story:

One time, Ada attended a gathering where some people doubted her abilities because she was a woman. Instead of feeling discouraged, she engaged them in a math discussion and impressed everyone with her knowledge! She showed them that brilliance knows no gender.

What Can We Learn from Ada?

Ada's story teaches us that:

- **Follow Your Passions:** If you love something, go for it! Don't let others tell you what you can or can't do.
- **Be Courageous:** Trying something new or challenging can be scary, but courage helps you push through fears.
- **Work Hard:** Success often comes from dedication and effort. Keep learning and growing.
- **Support Others:** Just like Ada's mother and mentors supported her, we can encourage our friends and family in their dreams.

Remember:

Ada Lovelace didn't let the challenges of her time stop her from making history. She showed that with passion and perseverance, you can overcome obstacles and achieve amazing things. Who knows what you might accomplish with the same determination?

Chapter 8

Ada's Lasting Impact

Inspiring Future Generations

Ada Lovelace's story doesn't end with her own amazing achievements. In fact, her influence has grown even stronger over the years, inspiring people all around the world!

For a long time, not many people knew about Ada's work. Her notes were tucked away in old books, waiting to be rediscovered. Then, as computers started to become a big part of our lives, historians found her writings and realized just how important they were. They recognized Ada as the world's **first computer programmer**!

Today, Ada is a shining example of what can happen when you combine imagination with hard work. She showed that **anyone** can make a difference, no matter their challenges or what others might think.

Ada's legacy inspires:

- **Future Scientists and Engineers:** Many people, especially girls, look up to Ada and see that they too can pursue careers in science, technology, engineering, and math (often called **STEM**).
- **Inventors and Creators:** Ada's ability to think outside the box encourages others to dream big and come up with new ideas that could change the world.
- **Lifelong Learne**

- **rs:** Ada loved learning new things throughout her life. She inspires us to stay curious and keep exploring, no matter how old we are.

Meet Some Modern Trailblazers:

- **Mae Jemison:** The first African-American woman astronaut to travel to space. She was inspired by pioneers like Ada to reach for the stars—literally!
- **Reshma Saujani:** Founder of "Girls Who Code," an organization that helps girls learn computer programming, following in Ada's footsteps.
- **You:** Yes, you! Who knows what amazing things you might achieve inspired by Ada's story?

Celebrating Ada Lovelace Day

Did you know that there's a special day dedicated just to Ada Lovelace? It's called **Ada Lovelace Day**, and it's celebrated every year on the **second Tuesday of October**!

What's Ada Lovelace Day All About?

Ada Lovelace Day is a global celebration of women in science, technology, engineering, and math. On this day, people around the world:

- **Share Stories:** They talk about amazing women in STEM who are making a difference.
- **Host Events:** Schools, museums, and organizations hold workshops, science fairs, and talks to inspire others.
- **Encourage Participation:** Everyone is invited to join in, learn something new, and maybe even try out a science experiment or coding project!

Why Is It Important?

Ada Lovelace Day reminds us that:

- **Diversity Matters:** When people of all backgrounds contribute, we get better ideas and solutions.
- **Breaking Barriers:** Just like Ada overcame challenges, we can work towards a world where everyone has the chance to succeed.

- **Inspiration for All:** Learning about role models like Ada can spark excitement and ambition in young minds—just like yours!

Fun Fact: The programming language **"Ada"** was named in her honor! It's used around the world in systems where safety and reliability are super important, like airplanes and medical equipment.

A Lasting Legacy

Ada Lovelace's impact is like a pebble dropped into a pond—the ripples keep spreading outwards. Her courage to explore new ideas continues to encourage people everywhere to push boundaries and think creatively.

Every time you use a computer, play a video game, or even read about the latest technology, a part of Ada's dream lives on. She imagined a future where machines could help us in incredible ways, and today, that future is our reality.

Remember:

- **Stay Curious:** Keep asking questions about how things work.
- **Be Creative:** Use your imagination to think of new ideas.

- **Believe in Yourself:** Just like Ada, you can achieve amazing things.

Who's Next?

Maybe one day, people will celebrate your achievements too! The world is full of possibilities, and you have the potential to make a difference.

Chapter 9

Fun Facts About Ada

Interesting Things You Might Not Know

Ready to discover some cool and surprising facts about Ada Lovelace? Let's dive into some interesting tidbits that make her story even more amazing!

1. She Had a Fascination with Flying Machines

- **Ada's Childhood Dream:** When Ada was just 12 years old, she became obsessed with the idea of flying. She studied birds and tried to design her own flying machine!
- **"Flyology":** She called her project "Flyology" and filled notebooks with sketches of wings and ideas on how humans could soar through the skies. Talk about thinking ahead of her time!

2. Ada Was the Daughter of a Famous Poet

- **Her Father Was Lord Byron:** Ada's dad was Lord George Gordon Byron, one of the most famous poets in history. His poems were like the hit songs of the 1800s!
- **A Mix of Art and Science:** Even though she never really knew her father, Ada inherited his creativity and combined it with her love for math and science.

3. She Loved Music and Art

- **A Talented Musician:** Ada played the piano and the harp. She believed that music and math were connected, and understanding one could help with the other.

- **Artistic Flair:** Ada enjoyed drawing and painting. She saw beauty in both the arts and sciences, proving you don't have to choose between them!

4. She Predicted Computer-Generated Music

- **Musical Machines:** Ada imagined that machines could one day compose complex and beautiful music. Today, computers can create songs and even help musicians write music!

5. Ada Had a Pet Cat Named Mrs. Puff

- **Feline Friend:** Ada loved animals and had a pet cat she affectionately named Mrs. Puff. She even wrote playful letters pretending to be from Mrs. Puff!

6. She Was a Countess

- **Lady Ada Lovelace:** When Ada married William King-Noel, she became the Countess of Lovelace. That's why we often call her Ada Lovelace.

7. Ada Was Friends with Famous Scientists and Writers

- **Charles Dickens:** Ada was friends with Charles Dickens, the author of classics like "Oliver Twist" and "A Christmas Carol." They enjoyed discussing literature and ideas.

- **Fascinating Conversations:** She loved meeting interesting people and sharing thoughts on science, art, and the future.

8. She Dealt with Health Challenges

- **Overcoming Illness:** Ada faced many health problems throughout her life, including measles and migraines. But she didn't let that stop her from pursuing her passions.

9. She Loved Puzzles and Secret Codes

- **Mystery Messages:** Ada and her friends sometimes wrote letters using secret codes and ciphers. It was like a real-life spy game!

10. Ada Had a Sense of Adventure

- **Horseback Riding:** She enjoyed riding horses and exploring the countryside. Ada loved the feeling of freedom and the wind in her hair.

11. A Computer Language Named After Her

- **The ADA Language:** In 1980, the U.S. Department of Defense named a new computer programming language "Ada" in her honor. It's used in systems that require reliability, like airplanes and satellites.

12. She Was a Visionary of Artificial Intelligence

- **Thinking Machines:** Ada wondered if machines could ever think or create on their own, ideas that are central to artificial intelligence today.

13. Ada's Favorite Flower Was the Forget-Me-Not

- **A Symbol of Remembrance:** She loved the delicate blue flowers, which symbolize true love and memories. They remind us not to forget her contributions!

14. She Lived During Exciting Times

- **The Age of Invention:** Ada lived during the Industrial Revolution, a time when many new inventions like steam trains and telegraphs were changing the world.

15. She Believed in Combining Imagination with Logic

- **Poetical Science:** Ada coined the term "poetical science" to describe her approach to math and science, blending creativity with logic to make new discoveries.

Decode a Secret Message!

Just like Ada loved secret codes, here's a fun challenge for you:

Secret Message:

20-8-1-14-11 25-15-21 6-15-18 18-5-1-4-9-14-7 1-2-15-21-20 1-4-1!

Hint: Each number represents a letter in the alphabet (A=1, B=2, C=3, ..., Z=26).

Can you decode the message?

Answer to the Secret Message:

T H A N K Y O U F O R R E A D I N G A B O U T A D A!

Isn't Ada's story filled with fascinating twists and turns? She was not only a brilliant mathematician but also a creative, curious, and adventurous person. Ada shows us that it's okay to have many interests and that combining them can lead to extraordinary things.

Remember: Keep exploring, stay curious, and who knows—you might discover some fun facts about yourself along the way!

Questions

Engage with Ada's World

Ready to dive deeper into Ada Lovelace's exciting world? Here are some fun activities you can try at home or in the classroom. Let's unleash your creativity, just like Ada did!

1. Create Your Own Code

- **What You'll Need:** Paper, pencils, and your imagination!
- **What to Do:**
    - Invent a secret code using numbers, symbols, or drawings.
    - Write a message to a friend using your code.
    - See if they can crack it!
- **Why It's Fun:** Ada loved secret codes and ciphers. This activity lets you become a coder and share secret messages just like Ada did.

2. Design a Flying Machine

- **What You'll Need:** Paper, crayons or markers, and craft materials like cardboard, straws, and tape.
- **What to Do:**
    - Draw a picture of your own flying machine.
    - Think about how it would work. Does it have wings like a bird or propellers like a helicopter?

- Build a model of your design using craft materials.
- **Why It's Fun:** Remember Ada's "Flyology" project? Now you can explore the world of flight just like she did!

3. Compose a Mechanical Poem

- **What You'll Need:** Paper and a pencil.
- **What to Do:**
  - Write a poem about machines, numbers, or inventions.
  - Try to include some of the things Ada loved, like mathematics or music.
- **Why It's Fun:** Ada was the daughter of a poet and had a creative spirit. Combining art and science can lead to amazing creations!

4. Learn Basic Coding with Scratch

- **What You'll Need:** A computer with internet access.
- **What to Do:**
  - Visit the Scratch website (scratch.mit.edu).
  - Try out some beginner tutorials to create your own interactive story or game.
- **Why It's Fun:** Coding is like giving instructions to a computer—just like Ada did with her algorithms!

5. Time Traveler Interview

- **What You'll Need:** Paper and a pencil.
- **What to Do:**
    - Imagine you could interview Ada Lovelace.
    - Write down five questions you'd like to ask her.
    - Swap with a friend and answer the questions as if you were Ada!
- **Why It's Fun:** This activity helps you think about Ada's life and ideas, and it's a great way to practice creative thinking.

6. Build a Simple Machine

- **What You'll Need:** Everyday items like cardboard tubes, rubber bands, paper clips, and small weights.
- **What to Do:**
    - Create a simple machine like a pulley, lever, or a basic gear system.
    - Experiment with how it works and what it can do.
- **Why It's Fun:** Exploring mechanics helps you understand the kinds of machines that fascinated Ada and Charles Babbage.

7. Ada's Timeline Challenge

- **What You'll Need:** Paper, markers, and ruler.
- **What to Do:**
    - Create a timeline of Ada's life events.

- Include important dates, inventions, and milestones.
- Decorate it with drawings and colors.
- **Why It's Fun:** Visualizing Ada's life helps you remember key moments and see how her experiences shaped her contributions.

8. Invent a Future Technology

- **What You'll Need:** Paper and drawing tools.
- **What to Do:**
  - Think about what technology might look like 100 years from now.
  - Draw or write about your invention.
  - Explain how it works and how it helps people.
- **Why It's Fun:** Just like Ada imagined future possibilities, you can let your imagination soar and maybe even inspire real future inventions!

Quiz Yourself!

How much have you learned about Ada Lovelace? Test your knowledge with this fun quiz! Remember, it's okay to look back at previous chapters if you need a hint.

Question 1:
What was Ada Lovelace's full name?

A) Ada King
B) Augusta Ada Byron

C) Ada Smith
D) Ada Johnson

Question 2:
Who was Ada's famous inventor friend?

A) Thomas Edison
B) Albert Einstein
C) Charles Babbage
D) Isaac Newton

Question 3:
What machine did Charles Babbage design that Ada wrote programs for?

A) The Analytical Engine
B) The Steam Engine
C) The Time Machine
D) The Flying Car

Question 4:
What is Ada Lovelace known as?

A) The First Astronaut
B) The Queen of England
C) The World's First Computer Programmer
D) The Inventor of the Telephone

Question 5:
What special day is celebrated in Ada's honor?

A) Ada Lovelace Day
B) International Math Day
C) Science Fiction Day
D) Computer Safety Day

Question 6:
What did young Ada try to design after studying birds?

A) A submarine
B) A flying machine
C) A robot
D) A musical instrument

Question 7:
What did Ada call her approach that combined creativity and science?

A) Magical Math
B) Poetical Science
C) Artistic Arithmetic
D) Scientific Poetry

Question 8:
What language was named after Ada Lovelace?

A) Python
B) Java
C) Ada
D) Ruby

Question 9:
Which of these was one of Ada's hobbies?

A) Skateboarding
B) Coding video games
C) Horseback riding
D) Cooking exotic foods

Question 10:
True or False: Ada Lovelace wrote her notes in the 21st century.

Answers:

1. **B) Augusta Ada Byron**
2. **C) Charles Babbage**
3. **A) The Analytical Engine**
4. **C) The World's First Computer Programmer**
5. **A) Ada Lovelace Day**
6. **B) A flying machine**
7. **B) Poetical Science**
8. **C) Ada**
9. **C) Horseback riding**
10. **False** (She wrote her notes in the 19th century)

How Did You Do?

- **8-10 Correct:** Amazing! You're an Ada Lovelace expert!
- **5-7 Correct:** Great job! You know a lot about Ada.
- **1-4 Correct:** Good effort! You might enjoy re-reading some chapters to learn more.

Keep Exploring!

Remember, the spirit of learning and curiosity is what made Ada Lovelace so special. Keep asking questions, trying new things, and dreaming big. Who knows what incredible things you'll discover?

Glossary

Key Terms Explained

Welcome to the Glossary! Here you'll find easy and fun explanations of some special words and ideas from Ada's amazing story. Let's explore together!

Algorithm

- **What It Means:** A set of step-by-step instructions to solve a problem or complete a task.
- **Why It's Cool:** Think of an algorithm like a recipe for baking cookies! Just as you follow steps to make yummy treats, computers follow algorithms to do things like play games or solve math problems.

Analytical Engine

- **What It Means:** A super-smart machine designed by Charles Babbage that could be programmed to perform different calculations.
- **Why It's Cool:** It's like the great-great-grandparent of today's computers! Ada wrote the first program for this machine, imagining all the amazing things it could do.

Bernoulli Numbers

- **What It Means:** Special numbers in mathematics used for complex calculations.
- **Why It's Cool:** Ada wrote a program to calculate these tricky numbers, showing how brilliant she was at math!

Charles Babbage

- **Who He Is:** A famous mathematician and inventor who became Ada's good friend.
- **Why He's Important:** He designed the Difference Engine and the Analytical Engine, and together with Ada, they dreamed up ideas that led to modern computers.

Computer Program

- **What It Means:** A set of instructions that tells a computer what to do.
- **Why It's Cool:** Without programs, computers wouldn't know how to do anything! Ada wrote the world's first one.

Difference Engine

- **What It Means:** A mechanical calculator invented by Charles Babbage that could perform specific mathematical tasks.

- **Why It's Cool:** It was one of the earliest machines designed to do math automatically, paving the way for future computers.

Engineer

- **What It Means:** A person who designs, builds, or fixes machines, structures, or systems.
- **Why It's Cool:** Engineers create the things that make our world work, from bridges and airplanes to computers and robots!

Flyology

- **What It Means:** Ada's made-up word for her study of flying when she was a kid.
- **Why It's Cool:** At just 12 years old, Ada tried to design a flying machine. Talk about big dreams!

Imagination

- **What It Means:** The ability to think of new ideas or picture things that aren't real (yet!).
- **Why It's Cool:** Ada used her imagination to envision machines and inventions far ahead of her time.

Industrial Revolution

- **What It Means:** A period in history when many new machines and inventions changed the way people lived and worked.
- **Why It's Cool:** It was an exciting time of innovation, and Ada was right in the middle of it!

Legacy

- **What It Means:** Something handed down from the past, like ideas or achievements that people remember.
- **Why It's Cool:** Ada's legacy inspires us to be curious and creative, just like she was.

Mathematician

- **What It Means:** A person who studies and works with math.
- **Why It's Cool:** Mathematicians help us understand the world, from counting stars to creating video games!

Mechanics

- **What It Means:** The branch of science that deals with how things move and work.
- **Why It's Cool:** Understanding mechanics helped Ada and Charles design their incredible machines.

Programmer

- **What It Means:** Someone who writes instructions (programs) for computers to follow.
- **Why It's Cool:** Programmers can create apps, games, websites, and all sorts of cool technology. Ada was the very first one!

Punched Cards

- **What It Means:** Cards with holes punched in them used to tell early machines what to do.
- **Why It's Cool:** They were like the USB drives of the 1800s! The patterns of holes acted as instructions for machines like the Analytical Engine.

Steam Engine

- **What It Means:** A machine that uses steam to create power.
- **Why It's Cool:** Steam engines powered trains and factories during Ada's time, making travel and work much faster.

Technology

- **What It Means:** Tools, machines, or systems that help solve problems or make life easier.
- **Why It's Cool:** Technology is all around us—from smartphones to rockets—and it all started with ideas from pioneers like Ada!

Visionary

- **What It Means:** A person who thinks about or plans for the future with imagination and wisdom.
- **Why It's Cool:** Ada was a visionary who imagined computers doing amazing things long before they existed.

Algorithm (Again!)

- **Wait a Minute:** Didn't we already define this? Yes! But it's so important and cool that it's worth mentioning twice.

Poetical Science

- **What It Means:** Ada's idea of combining creativity and imagination with math and science.
- **Why It's Cool:** She showed that being artistic and scientific can go hand-in-hand, leading to incredible discoveries.

Curiosity

- **What It Means:** A strong desire to learn or know something.
- **Why It's Cool:** Curiosity is like a superpower that leads to new ideas and inventions. Ada's curiosity helped her change the world!

Innovation

- **What It Means:** Creating new ideas, products, or ways of doing things.
- **Why It's Cool:** Innovations make our lives better, and anyone can be an innovator—even you!

Computing

- **What It Means:** The process of using computers to solve problems or perform tasks.
- **Why It's Cool:** Computing is at the heart of so many things we use today, like video games, apps, and even space travel!

Ada Lovelace Day

- **What It Means:** A special day to celebrate Ada's life and all the amazing women in science, technology, engineering, and math.
- **Why It's Cool:** It's a day to inspire everyone to explore and enjoy STEM subjects, just like Ada did.

Remember:

This glossary is here to help you understand and enjoy the wonderful world of Ada Lovelace. Keep exploring, stay curious, and never stop asking questions!

Timeline of Ada's Life

Important Dates and Events

Join us on a magical journey through the life of **Ada Lovelace**, the amazing girl who dreamed up the first computer program! Let's explore the key moments that made her story so inspiring.

1815 - A Star is Born

- **December 10: Augusta Ada Byron** is born in London, England.
- Her parents are the famous poet **Lord Byron** and mathematician **Lady Annabella Milbanke Byron**.
- Ada is their only child together.

1816 - Early Changes

- **April:** Ada's father, Lord Byron, leaves England forever when Ada is just a few months old.
- Ada is raised by her mother, who encourages her interest in math and science.

1828 - Dreaming of Flight

- **Age 12:** Ada becomes fascinated with flying machines.
- She studies birds and designs her own plans for a flying device, calling her project **"Flyology"**.

- Ada sketches wings and imagines soaring through the sky!

1833 - Meeting a Genius

- **June:** At **age 17**, Ada attends a party where she meets **Charles Babbage**, a brilliant inventor.
- Charles shows her his **Difference Engine**, a machine that can perform calculations.
- Ada is captivated, and a lifelong friendship begins.

1835 - Love and Family

- **July 8:** Ada marries **William King**, becoming **Lady Ada King**.
- William later becomes the **Earl of Lovelace**, making Ada the **Countess of Lovelace**.
- They have three children: **Byron**, **Anne Isabella (Annabella)**, and **Ralph Gordon**.

1838 - Becoming Countess of Lovelace

- William is officially made the **Earl of Lovelace**.
- Ada is now known as **Countess Ada Lovelace**.

1842-1843 - Writing History

- Ada translates an article about Charles Babbage's new invention, the **Analytical Engine**, from French to English.

- She adds her own extensive **"Notes"**, which are longer than the original article!
- In her notes, Ada writes the **first computer program**, an algorithm to calculate **Bernoulli numbers**.
- She imagines future possibilities for machines beyond just math.

1843 - A Visionary's Insight

- Ada publishes her translated article with notes in an English science journal.
- She predicts that machines could create music, art, and more by following instructions.
- Ada's ideas lay the groundwork for modern computing.

1852 - A Fond Farewell

- **November 27:** Ada passes away at the young age of **36** due to illness.
- She is buried next to her father, Lord Byron, in **Nottinghamshire**, England.
- Though her life was short, her impact is everlasting.

1980 - Honoring Her Legacy

- The **U.S. Department of Defense** names a new computer programming language "**Ada**" in her honor.
- This language is used in systems where safety is critical, like airplanes and medical devices.

2009 - Ada Lovelace Day Begins

- The first **Ada Lovelace Day** is celebrated to honor her contributions to computing and to encourage girls and women in STEM (Science, Technology, Engineering, and Mathematics).
- It's celebrated every year on the **second Tuesday of October**.

Highlights of Ada's Incredible Journey

- **A Bright Beginning:** Born to a poet and a mathematician, Ada combined creativity and logic from the start.
- **A Mind That Soared:** From designing flying machines to envisioning computers, her imagination knew no bounds.
- **Friendship with Babbage:** Her collaboration with Charles Babbage led to groundbreaking ideas in computing.
- **Pioneer Programmer:** Writing the first computer algorithm, she became the world's **first computer programmer**.
- **Inspiration for All:** Ada's life encourages us to be curious, creative, and courageous.

Fun Activity: Make Your Own Timeline!

Just like Ada's timeline, you can create one for your own life.

Here's How:

1. **List Important Events:**
    - Your birthday.
    - First day of school.
    - Learning to ride a bike.
    - A memorable family trip.
    - Any special achievements or fun moments.
2. **Draw It Out:**
    - Use a long piece of paper.
    - Mark the dates and write a short description of each event.
    - Add drawings, stickers, or photos to make it colorful.
3. **Share Your Story:**
    - Show your timeline to family and friends.
    - Talk about your favorite memories and what you look forward to in the future.

Remember:

Ada Lovelace showed us that with imagination and determination, we can achieve amazing things. Your timeline is just the beginning of your own exciting journey!

Keep Dreaming Big!

Who knows? Maybe one day, your life will inspire others, just like Ada's inspires us.

Made in United States
Troutdale, OR
04/10/2025